The Dalmation or Coach Dog
His Supposed Origin with Practical Information As To His Qualities

by H. Fred Lauer

with an introduction by Jackson Chambers

This work contains material that was originally published in 1902.

This publication is within the Public Domain.

*This edition is reprinted for educational purposes
and in accordance with all applicable Federal Laws.*

Self Reliance Books

Get more historic titles on animal and stock breeding, gardening and old fashioned skills by visiting us at:

Introduction

I am pleased to present this reprinted edition of Mr. H. Fred Lauer's famous book "The Dalmation or Coach Dog". The book was first published in 1902 and contains the very early history of this breed. Prior to its release, no other book was available on the Dalmation, nor was another written for many years after.

As with all reprinted books of this age that are intended to perfectly reproduce the original edition, considerable pains and effort had to be undertaken to correct fading and sometimes outright damage to existing proofs of this title. At times, this task is quite monumental, requiring an almost total "rebuilding" of some pages from digital proofs of multiple copies. Despite this, imperfections still sometimes exist in the final proof and may detract from the visual appearance of the text.

I hope you enjoy reading this book as much as I enjoyed re-publishing and making it available to fanciers again.

With Regards,

Jackson Chambers

Very truly yours

H. Fred Lauer,

THE DALMATIAN

THE PROBABLE ORIGIN.

Very little is known of the origin of this dog or what country first gave him birth. It is a mystery to the writer why it can't be traced back, and yet I suppose he is too old a dog to go back several hundred years. This I persume has not and never will be found out.

Some early writers inform us that he first came from Spain and Jardine, in his "Naturalist's Library," mentions a picture of a spotted dog, time the middle of the sixteenth century, from which he believes our modern Dalmatian must have been descended. Another writer informs us that this dog came originally from Bengal, where his peculiar markings made him much admired by the wealthy and luxurious natives, whose establishments were not complete without several spotted dogs in the kennels or about the stable.

Stonehendge, in his last edition of the "Dogs of the British Islands," gives it as his opinion that the Dalmatian is a Pointer when at home, and some of the early Dalmatians and early Pointers were very much alike.

Again, we are informed that this dog was used in Denmark to draw carts and other conveyances utilized by the thrifty Dane and his wife to take their commodities from place to place. Moreover it was commonly supposed that the dogs had originally been obtained from a cross with a tiger. This I doubt very much, and leaving the above statement for what it is worth and coming to more modern instances, we have our common Dalmatian or "Coach" dog likened to a Pointer.

Dalziel thinks it reasonable to assume its native home was Dalmatia, on the eastern shores of the Gulf of Venice, and a province in the southern part of Austria. Of whatever family or habitat, the badge of its tribe has always been the spotted coat.

We are also informed that the Dalmatian was a dog of war, stood sentinel on the borders of Dalmatia and Croatia, and was

3

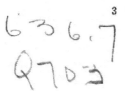

attached to the farthest outposts to give warning to the Turk. This story goes on to add with such a neat play of words that one doubts whether they fit history or history has been made to fit them. It may be that the old war discipline remains to this day in the capacity of the Dalmatian of being trained to the gun. It is a capacity not sufficiently exploited in England or America, although in their native land these dogs were used as pointers.

THE DALMATIAN
From a painting by Reinagle

Note the "Wall" eye and cropped ears, also running gear.

Other expert opinions go to show that the sporting instinct is probably latent in the Dalmatian, but not absolutely dead. While it is not improbable that the breed was originally used for sporting purposes, and indeed, their appearance seems to indicate that generations ago they sprang from some of the branches of the Pointer family, still so long a time has elapsed since these conditions that they seem to have completely lost their noses. Mrs.

Boucher says: "We have used them for partridge shooting and found them very fair pointers, and they retrieve well."

Who first mentioned the Dalmatian we have not found out and don't think we ever will, therefore it is useless to write on this subject any further. Having thus drawn the track of the Dalmatian across two continents from Copenhagen to Calcutta, I

"Kiefer," a prize winner on the bench, and in the first road trial held in America. He is a son of Polka Dot ex Teddy L. and sires liver spotted pups. Owned by H. Fred Lauer.

leave the choice of the allocating its place of maturity to the wisdom or fancy of the reader.

There is little doubt that our modern Dalmatian sprang from Dalmatia, hence his name "Dalmatian," which alone should convince us. However, at the present time it matters not what country first gave him birth.

Polka Dot, at one time a bench winner but now used for breeding, is a very good matron and produces excellent puppies. Owned by H. Fred Lauer.

Ch. Spotted Diamond of Edgecomb Kennels, Chestnut Hill, Pa., as well as being a show specimen, she is an elegant worker with a team.

THE DALMATIAN IN AMERICA.

The Dalmatian has been with us centuries and is with us now and will stay with us, although the past fifteen years there were not many to be seen anywhere in America, until five years ago when several enthusiastic fanciers took to this beautiful breed and with hard work and energy bred and brought

Champion Gedney Farm Roadster. Noted for his distinct markings, and good head. Sire of Gedney Farm Surprise and Gedney Sportsman: two of America's best puppies.

before the public that almost lost breed of dog and companion to man—the Dalmatian. Not until the year of 1896 were classes opened at eastern shows with very little support until four years ago when with some home bred ones and some imported ones the entries were very good.

One comes to the conclusion that the progress made by the Dalmatian is little short of marvelous; the improvement in the Dalmatian himself and the strides he has made in public favor have been quite exceptional, and in the four years just past the

Dalmatian may fairly claim to have been more in the public eye than ever before.

The entries at nearly all the principal shows have been not only strong in numbers, but what is far more important, have been excellent in quality, and some cases indeed as at New York, Philadelphia, Wissahickon, and several others, the winners have been difficult to separate especially at Philadelphia in 1905 and New York and Wissahickon in 1906. At Wissahickon two

Ch. Rockcliffe Buck Shot. Owned by John W. Minturn, New York.

of the best bitches in this country, Ch. Spotted Diamond and Gedney Farm Dreadnought, met in open and winners classes, the former defeating the latter under Mr. Terry as Judge. Ch. Rockcliffe Runaway is supposed to be the best Dalmatian in America today, although he is an imported one, he has been beaten by a home bred one, Ch. King at New York in 1906.

We have a great many more good dogs and bitches, also some promising puppies. With careful breeding and a little more enthusiasm on the part of the fanciers, there is a great future for the American-bred Dalmatian. I did not expect, years ago, that the Dalmatian would become so popular, or that in such a comparatively short time become so vastly improved. In fact, none of us thought in those days that the Dalmatian in America would ever win such universal recognition, and acknowledged position, in the dog world as he holds today.

Dalmatians worthy of the name as we understand them today were very few ten or fifteen years ago, but at the present day we have a few in nearly all parts of the country.

THE DALMATIAN CLUB.

In the year 1904 enthusiastic breeders and fanciers of this scarce variety of dog, got together and formed a club whose sole ambition and object is the perpetuation of the Dalmatian and to increase his fading fortunes. Its purpose is novel to say the least and the organization will be the only one of its kind in America. The name of the club is "The Dalmatian Club of America." It is established with a view to promote the breeding of pure Dalmatians; to define precisely and publish a definition of the true type; and to urge the adoption of such type on breeders, fanciers, Judges, dog show committees, etc., as the only recognized and unvarying standard by which Dalmatians ought to be judged, which may in the future be uniformly accepted as the sole standard

9

of excellence in breeding and in awarding prizes of merit to Dalmatians and (giving prizes, supporting shows, and taking other steps) to do all in its power to protect and advance the interest of the breed. The Officers of the club at the time of its organization were: President, Alfred B. Maclay; Vice President, H. T. Peters; Secretary and Treasurer, J. Sergeant Price, Jr. The latter being an ardent admirer and breeder of the Dalmatian and the founder of this club.

The Officers elected for 1907, were: President, J. Sergeant Price, Jr.; Vice President, Howard Willets; Secretary and Treasurer, D. C. Sands, Jr.; Board of Governors are the Officers and H. T. Peters, Henry Jarrett, Alfred B. Maclay, and Joseph B. Thomas, Jr.

A string of Gedney Farm Dogs. Owned by Howard Willets, White Plains, N. Y. The largest and best Dalmatian Kennel in America.

It started out with twenty-six members, and now it has an enrollment of forty-six members, and to-day is one of the strongest specialty clubs in America. It has given a generous list of specials at all the prominent shows. It is the intention of this club to promote dog shows of its own, at which the center of attraction shall be the Dalmatian.

The American Dalmatian Club is in good hands and in excellent condition, and what is now necessary for its continued success is a continuation of the same spirit of enterprise which has characterized its management during its duration to foster the breed.

It has not the easy road to success that so many clubs have had, with a membership of probably a hundred or more at hand, without the asking, for the admirers and supporters of this beautiful breed are by no means numerous and will require to be largely recruited before it is likely to be on secure footing, for in all clubs there are always some members that are like seed that fall on stony ground and they form a percentage that has to be overcome by hard work on the part of those who can get in new additions. The wonderful good given the breed by the club is an excellent illustration of what can be done and accomplished by a specialty club, which goes to work in a sportsmanlike manner, to do all in its power to encourage members, breeders and fanciers to advance the interest of the breed. A glance over the names of members of this club will show you one of the best list of members of any Specialty Club in America. Prominent horse and dog men and women, and people in every walk of life are in it for the sport it affords and not for the money. The following are the members of The Dalmatian Club of America:—

MEMBERS.

Fred. Appleton, White Plains, N. Y.
Mrs. Hastings Arnold, Jr., East Williston, Long Island, N. Y.
Mrs. Edward Atkins, 309 High St., Germantown, Philadelphia, Pa.
Mrs. Aurel Batonyi, Newport, R. I.
C. Perry Beadleston, 25 E. 51st St., New York, N. Y.
Mrs. Charles F. Cartledge, 379 Washington St., Brooklyn, N. Y.
J. F. Carlisle, 20 Broad St., New York, N. Y.
R. F. Carman, Huntington, Long Island, N. Y.
F. Ambrose Clark, Westbury, Long Island, N. Y.
M. F. Dalton, Florence, N. J.
G. Howard Davison, Millbrook, Duchess Co., N. Y.
Mrs. C. F. Dennee, 195 Bellevue St., Longwood, Boston, Mass.
Percy R. Drury, 195 Bellevue St., Longwood, Boston, Mass.
S. E. Gallagher, New Brighton, Penna.
H. L. Herbert, 15 Church St., New York, N. Y.
Miss Rachel C. Holmes, Covington, Ky.
H. H. Hunnewell, Wellesley, Mass.
Dr. Henry Jarrett, The Pascoe, Philadelphia, Pa.
Miss Edith M. Kennedy, New York, N. Y.
H. Fred Lauer, Ashland, Penna.
Arnold Lawson, 32 State St., Boston, Mass.
Herbert Floyd, 107 E. 69th St., New York, N. Y.
Alfred B. Maclay, 358 Fifth Ave., New York, N. Y.
Miss M. W. Martin, Chestnut Hill, Philadelphia, Penna.
Miss Doris Mather, 110 Waterman St., Providence, R. I.
E. Rittenhouse Miller, 143 E. Mt. Airy Ave., Mt. Airy, Philadelphia, Pa.
John W. Minturn, 537 Fifth Ave., New York, N. Y.
Clarence Moore, Prides Crossing, Mass.
P. A. McHattie, Beaver Falls, Penna.
H. T. Peters, 1 Broadway, New York, N. Y.

Dalmatian bitch heavily marked, has spotted tail and although very dark
is attractive. She is a litter sister to Polka Dot and owned by W. S.
Zimmerman, Shamokin, Pa.

Ch. Edgecomb D'Artagnan, an American bred one, is a good type and has
conformation to stand road work. He is a grand sire of well marked
puppies.

S. Osgood Pell, 537 Fifth Ave., New York, N. Y.
Mrs. Charles Pfizer, 19 W. 50 St., New York, N. Y.
J. Sergeant Price, Jr., Chestnut Hill, Philadelphia, Penna.
Daniel C. Sands, Jr., Kensico, N. Y.
Thomas H. Terry, 380 Main St., Norfolk, Va.
Joseph B. Thomas, Jr., 1 Madison Ave., New York, N. Y.
Mrs. M. A. Todd, New Brighton, Penna.
R. C. Vanderbilt, Sandy Point Farm, Newport, R. I.
R. H. Williams, Jr., 1 Broadway, New York, N. Y.
F. Fred. Willis, 31 E. Russell St., Columbus, Ohio.
Howard Willets, White Plains, N. Y.
Mrs. F. D. Wyckoff, 23 W. 57th St., New York, N. Y.
F. L. Wilson, 170 Broadway, Long Branch, N. J.

The following is a description and standard recommended by the American Dalmatian Club, and is that of the English Dalmatian Club, but is not one to the liking of a great many members of the club, and we hope in the future it will have various changes, for it is not at all suitable for the purpose of letting a novice know what is wanted or needed in a true type Dalmatian.

THE STANDARD.

"The Head should be of a fair length, the skull flat, rather broad between the ears, and moderately well defined at the temples,

Imported Ch. Pearlette owned by Alfred B. Maclay, New York City.

13

Champion Queen Belle and Ch. Windy Valley Snowstorm, owned by Percy R. Drury, of Longwood, Boston, Mass., Queen Belle is one of America's best bitches, and wins in hot company.

i.e. exhibiting a moderate amount of stop, and not in one straight line from the nose to the occiput bone as required in a Bull Terrier. It should be entirely free from wrinkle.

"The Muzzle should be long and powerful; the lips clean, fitting the jaw moderately close.

"The Eyes should be set moderately well apart, and of medium size, round, bright and sparkling, with an intelligent expression, their color greatly depending on the markings of the dog. In the black spotted variety the eyes should be dark (black or brown); in the liver-spotted variety they should be light (yellow or light brown). Wall eyes are permissible.

"The rim around the Eyes in the black-spotted variety should be black; in the liver-spotted variety brown—never flesh-colored in either.

"The Ears should be set on rather high, of moderate size, rather wide at the base and gradually tapering to a rounded point. They should be carried close to the head, be thin and fine in texture, and always spotted, the more profusely the better.

"The Nose in the black-spotted variety should always be black, in the liver-spotted variety always brown.

14

"Neck and Shoulders.—The Neck should be fairly long, nicely arched, light and tapering, and entirely free from throatiness. The Shoulders should be moderately oblique, clean and muscular, denoting speed.

"Body, Back, Chest and Loins.—The Chest should not be too wide, but very deep and capacious, ribs moderately well sprung, never rounded like barrel hoops (which would indicate want of speed). The Back powerful; Loin strong, muscular and slightly arched.

"Legs and Feet, of great importance. The fore-legs should be perfectly straight, strong and heavy in bone; elbows close to the

Imported Windy Valley Benrino. A strong vigorous dog.

body; feet compact with well arched toes, and tough elastic pads. In the hind legs the muscles should be clean, though well defined; the hocks well let down.

"Nails, in the black-spotted variety, black and white; in the liver-spotted variety, brown and white.

"The Tail should not be too long, strong at the insertion and gradually tapering towards the end, free from coarseness. It should not be inserted too low down, but carried with a slight

15

curve upwards, and never curled. It should be spotted, the more profusely the better.

"The Coat short, hard, dense and fine, sleek and glossy in appearance, but neither woolly nor silky.

"Color and Markings.—These are most important points. The ground color in both varieties should be pure white, very decided, and not intermixed. The color of the spots in the black-spotted variety should be black, the deeper and richer the black the better; in the liver-spotted variety they should be brown. The spots should not intermingle, but be as round and well-defined as

Gedney Farm Surprise. A grand young dog, who, no doubt, will be an American bred champion.

possible, the more distinct the better; in size they should be from that of a dime to a half dollar. The spots on the head, face, ears, legs, tail and extremities to be smaller than those on the body.

"Size.—Height of Dogs and Bitches between 19 and 23 inches.

"Weight.—Between 35 and 50 pounds.

"General Appearance.—The Dalmatian should represent a strong muscular and active dog, symmetrical in outline and free from coarseness and lumber, capable of great endurance with a fair amount of speed.

Ch. Runaway, the international champion, considered the best dog in America. Owned by John Minturn, New York City.

STANDARD OF EXCELLENCE.

Head and eyes 10
Ears, ... 5
Neck and shoulders, ... 10
Body, back, chest and loins, ... 10
Legs and feet, ... 15
Coat, ... 5
Color and markings, ... 30
Tail, ... 5
Size, symmetry, etc., ... 10

    Grand total, ... 100

Dalmatians owned by P. A. McHattie, Beaver Falls Pa. The centre dog is Ch. King.

Duke of Norfolk, owned by Indian Neck Farm, Oakdale, L .I.

18

DESCRIPTION OF THE DALMATIAN.

The Dalmatian has not up until the past eight years proved particularly popular with the general public. He has been left to the care of the servant, and children called him the plum-pudding dog. He has not deserved such treatment, for there is no other breed of dog more suitable for an all round dog than the Dalmatian. It has always been a mystery to me why this breed of

Imported Gedney Farm Bucklow. A large spotted dog, deep in color with very black ears.

dog has not become more popular, because a good specimen is undoubtedly a very handsome dog, and I have heard more than one owner say that as a companion the Dalmatian has not many superiors. He is capable of showing strong attachment to his master and will not make friends with every Tom, Dick and Harry that comes along. He is by no means an easy dog to coax away from home, by strangers, nor even by those who are around him

19

at various times. One very good habit they have and that is this, when you want them, you need not go chasing all over the neighborhood to find them, they are not a dog to wander around, but are always at home and ready at any moment to go for a walk or run with their master, which they enjoy very much.

In describing these dogs as a house dog or carriage dog (which I will dwell on later) or constant companion, for someone who wants a "dog" they have less objectionable qualities and less objectionably marked characteristics that would get them into

Rex, owned by J. Sergeant Price, Jr., years ago was a nice marked dog, and a good coacher. This dog shows ears that were black when born, and were not objected to at that time.

trouble with their neighbors than any dog I could mention, and they have the faculty, which is not to be lightly overlooked in our daily companion, viz; that of minding their own business, though they are fine watch dogs. They will not make friends with other breeds of dogs and follow them all over the land, therefore, they are always at home except when out with their master.

Our Dalmatian makes a very affectionate companion; he is kindly in disposition, by no means quarrelsome, and cleanly in his habits. They are good ratters where a large dog can move. With children they are most good tempered and affectionate. I am informed of one instance in particular in New York where he ran far ahead of the fire engine in an East Side street filled with children and dragged a little cripple from under the very hoofs of the rushing fire horses. It would seem if ever these dogs are bred in

Rube, owned by Harry G. Trathen, Ashland, Pa. This dog is trained to do tricks, and is very intelligent, also a good coacher, having won second at York in 1906. Head markings objected to by most fanciers.

anything like numbers, they are bound to increase and be taken up freely.

The Dalmatian is a level headed dog and certainly intelligent and capable of learning a great deal. He can be taught many things. He often appears and assists to earn his master's living by performing on the stage, where many good ones are to be seen. "Idstone" tells us of a celebrated performing dog of this variety which acted as a clown, and the best of the kind he ever saw. At the Farm Show in New York an entire troupe of performing Dalmatians were to be seen.

THE DALMATIAN COACH DOG.

One of the most prevailing passions of our Dalmatian is their innate love for horses, and the stable is their choice, and for this faculty and predilection they owe much of the esteem in which they are held by those who own them. Almost invariably have we seen them about some stable, yet this is what might be expected, for, whoever brought them from abroad, it is fair to assume that they were mainly coachmen or grooms and the dogs went with them to their stables.

The Dalmatian differs this much from other dogs. His

Ch. Spotted Diamond, ch. D'Artagnan, Sneezer and Spot, coaching under a coach owned by J. Sergeant Price, Jr., Chestnut Hill, Pa. Very few "champions" are used in this manner.

attachment is for the stable, horse, carriage and his master; other dogs make friends with the human race entirely. He is fond of the horses, lives in the stable with them, is little or no trouble to the grooms, and the coachman does not think his master's equipage perfect, unless it has a nicely spotted dog running under the front axle of the carriage, wagon or coach, or close to the horses' heels. He has become purely and simply the dog of the stable; and the friend of the horse and his master. His affection

Gedney Farm Dogs at daily exercise. Note how
close these dogs run to the horses heels.

Mr. J. Sergeant Price, Jr's. four of grays and his well appointed road coach
with a team of Dalmatians under the front axle.   Mr. Price deserves
credit for having well broken dogs for road work.

for the horse is unlimited, and it is a fact that the Dalmatian, because of constant association with the surroundings of the stable, is difficult to coax therefrom.

Their unique appearance and great ability to run made them very popular with the travelers from England and the continent, who in time of travel by coach and horse, passed through Dalmatia and those in need of a companion or dog to guard them on their journey, saw quickly that this dog was particularly adapted to their wants. Sporting prints, depicting coaching scenes, which bear the

Imported Gedney Farm Sandstorm. A prize winning liver spotted Dalmatian

date of the eighteenth century, have Dalmatian dogs running with the horses. Hence he can be found all over the world to-day used in the same manner, and he makes himself useful in taking good care of valuable blankets, robes and whips, when his master leaves the team; at this post, he is very cross, especially to strangers. As this dog has been connected with the stables, horses, coaches and travelers for centuries he is commonly alluded to as a "Coach

24

Dog." By this he is known all over the world to-day—more so than by Dalmatian.

Another reason why he is called "Coach Dog" is that he is mostly seen running ahead, or along the side, or under the front axle of vehicles. Some people prefer him to run ahead like the fire engine Dalmatians do, others want them under the hind axle so his tail can be seen from the back, others want him close to the horses' heels while others claim the dog in that

Imported Gedney Farm Dreadnought. A well marked bitch, and an elegant brood bitch. She is the Dam of Sportsman and Surprise.

position gets too dirty and ruins his ears and eyes by the dust and dirt thrown by the horses' hoofs. He is used for many purposes; with a team, to follow on horseback, under single, double and four; to jump in and guard the carriage, to go in front when standing and watch the horses, or to lie down under the carriage when standing. His ability and working qualities about an equipage may be another reason why he is known as "Coach Dog."

There is a great deal of dispute as to where the proper position is for a coach dog. One would think under the carriage or close to the horses' heels, as when a dog is in any other position every "cur" will run and snap at him which will end in a scrap, as a Dalmatian will take his own part when attacked invariably minding his own business. It has been said that the Dalmatian obtained a reputation for stupidity, which it did not deserve. He seems to have inbred in him a love for a horse and stable—the former his friend, the latter his home. This attribute has led many to think him a rough, stupid dog, but this is not the

Mr. Percy Drury and Ch. Snowstorm. This is a suitable conveyance to train a Dalmatian to coach.

case, as he shows uncommon skill and sagacity in keeping close to the horses' heels or underneath the front axle of the carriage in the busiest and most crowded thoroughfares, and is seldom or never lost. A dog capable of doing such work is not lacking in brains and this is not the work of a stupid dog by any means. At this post he feels perfectly safe when other dogs run at him to attack him.

This habit of running out at every vehicle and barking, which most dogs have, is very annoying and I do not know of one instance that a Dalmatian got into the habit of doing this. Running underneath the vehicle, or "Coaching" as it is called, seems to be a characteristic formed by heredity in a Dalmatian, as most Dalmatians take to this place themselves, even puppies when only a few months old will go under the vehicle without the least training, and being kept with the horses all the time and going with the team, will soon find their way up behind the horses' heels, where one would think it impossible that the horse would not strike them on the head with his hoofs every

Gedney Farm Sportsman. Litter brother to Gedney Farm Surprise, but not so good.

step he takes. I have seen some Dalmatians get so nervous when the horse would walk, that he would run beside the horses' hind leg. This they do because they delight to go fast, and with some the faster the better they enjoy it. Most Dalmatians take to this themselves, while others are like black sheep in a flock and will never learn.

To train a Dalmatian to coach well is to train him when a puppy, take him out with the team and never go faster than a

An American bred bitch at nine months, out of Lillie ex ch. Runaway. Bred and owned by Mrs. Hastings Arnold, Jr., East Williston, Long Island, New York.

walk for a few times. A cart is a suitable conveyance for his first lessons, as you can best get him to come close to the horse and you can talk to him and encourage him. After this use a four wheeled vehicle. He may not come up so close to the horse at first, but gradually he will get up further, but don't expect it in a day, a week, or two weeks. Some people get over anxious to have them run close and tie them to the front axle. This is not advisable as they may pull back and then you drag them, and they may be spoiled for ever. A better plan, if they do not come up, take a light cord about six or seven yards long, attach it to the collar of the dog, then under the vehicle, up over the dasher; hold the cord, giving the dog slack, start the horse on a walk, and if the dog comes up, take up the slack so he does not tread in it, if he should pull back do not try to hold him, give him plenty of slack and then pull on him by degrees and coax him up. In this way you do not drag him and you won't spoil him. Another good way is to take him along with a trained dog several times and the puppy will soon learn to go under with the older dog, especially when other dogs run at him. There are men who make it a business of training Dalmatians to coach.

ROAD TRIALS.

Trials for Dalmatians have been talked about many times. At Wissahickon, 1906, an opportunity was given to those who claimed to have well broken coach dogs. Mr. J. Sergeant Price, Jr., an ardent admirer of working coach dogs, and secretary of the Wissahickon Kennel Club, opened a class for dogs and bitches (75 per cent. for their working ability under a carriage, behind a pair of horses, which was furnished at the ground, and 25 per cent. for their show qualities) for which an entry of seven resulted. The

Dr. George Pottiger, of Hamburg, Penna., with his coaching Dalmatian, Pottiger's Bell. She having won first prize in the road trial at York, Pa.

successful dogs were "Ponto," William Anson, Chestnut Hill, Penna.; "Kiefer," H. Fred Lauer, Ashland, Penna.; and "Pottigers Bell," Dr. Geo. Pottiger, Hamburg, Penna.

Wissahickon has the honor to say that they held the first Dalmatian Road Trial ever held in America, and one can say it proved successful, as it was the centre of attraction in the afternoon. The trial was judged by Mr. Thomas Terry. As the trial attracted so much attention at Wissahickon, it was decided to hold a trial at the York, Penna., show, which resulted in six entries. The equipage furnished was a handsome pair of Cobs to

29

Imported Gedney Farm Telegraph Duchess. Very black in spots, but inter-mixed. This kind make good bitches to breed to with a light marked dog.

a break wagon. I officiated as judge. Hundreds of people watched the spotted dogs show their wonderful skill in keeping close to the horses' heels while the horses trotted around the ring. Each dog ran by itself and a better lot of working Dalmatians never met in America before. The successful dogs were "Pottigers Bell" first, "Rube" second, "King" third, and "Gedney Farm Diamond" fourth. An exhibition trial was run, and the first, second and third prize dogs ran underneath at the one time. It was amusing to see how one dog would pass the other dog out in order to get close to the horses' heels. The enthused crowd applauded and cheered as they went around the ring several times, and one would think it impossible that the dogs did not meet with an accident, such as getting under the wheels or under the horses' hoofs.

Up to the time of this writing there have not been any rules adopted for coaching in Road Trials. The proper position fixed by the committee, and Judge for the trial was that the dog was to run as close as possible to the horses' heels, and stick to this post and not run out then back again. There is no doubt but what "close to the horses' heels," or underneath the front axle is the proper place for the dog, as most coachers take to this place as their choice. Watson says: "In the early seventies we remember a Dalmatian kept in a livery stable in Charles Street, New York, and this was the first dog they ever saw running between the horses when out with a carriage." The English style, when the dog was not running in advance, was for it to run underneath the carriage close to the horses' heels. The question of rules will no doubt be brought before the next meeting of the Dalmatian Club.

It has been customary in the British Isles to breed a rather large and heavy type of dog, but one fact alone precluded this line in America, viz., that our carriages are built closer to the ground than those in Great Britain and so if we wish to work our Dalmatians and keep them to what is now acknowledged to

Imported Ge..ney Farm Choice.   A large well marked dog, but with ears too black for body.

be their legitimate occupation—that of running under our vehicles —we must breed and select a dog of a size that is capable of doing this with a certain amount of ease and comfort to himself. So moderate sized Dalmatians should be the order of the dog in America.

THE MARKINGS.

The Dalmatian is a very handsome and striking dog with a snow white body, that should be as evenly and clearly marked as possible with black or liver spots. The two colors, may be on the same dog but should not mix or be mixed with white. Often

Dalmatian dogs owned by Miss Bonham, of York, Pa. The one on the left gives one an idea how dark some get, and it seems impossible that when born, he was white.

we see dogs on which the spots are mixed with much white. This makes the spots look bluish, and is called Huckleberry marking, and is not at all desirable. It often occurs that he has liver or tanned spots on his legs and about his neck.

The commonest color is the black spotted variety. The pure liver spotted are very scarce and it is a rare thing to see one at a show. Ch. Rockcliffe Goldspot, a beautiful liver spotted dog

Imported Rugby Brocade, a fine specimen of the Liver Spotted variety. She is a litter sister to Rugby Bombshell. Their mother was liver spotted, the sire black spotted.

Imported Ch. President, a good type liver spotted dog, winner of many prizes in England. Owned by Alfred B. Maclay, New York City.

who won the title of Champion in America, was the only one seen of late at the shows and was considered the best in America. His recent death was a severe blow to Mr. Minturn, his owner.

The spots are preferred from the size of a dime and running to about the size of a half dollar, but of whatever size, they must be clear, bright and distinct, also well defined and not too many so as to run together. Some dogs are marked with too much black on the head; some have large black patches over the whole side of the head, or on both sides and often joining each other on the top of the head, the ears are entirely black and they

Imported Rugby Bombshell, a liver spotted dog owned by Mrs. Hastings Arnold, Jr., of East Williston, Long Island, N. Y.

have too many spots on the face. Spotted ears are much preferred to black ears, the Standard says they should be always spotted. This I think is one of the oddities of "fancy," for present-day fanciers to think and to say that the Dalmatian must not have black ears, but should always be spotted. More than half of the Dalmatians we see at the shows have the black ear. Thirty years ago they had them. One hundred years ago they had them, and Reinagle's dog had them, so had Berwicks, centuries ago. At that time it was the custom to cut the ears off, but we do

34

not admire the cruel practice of depriving the poor animal of his
ears in order to increase beauty. Take our best dogs of to-day on
the bench and they have black ears, or so near black that they cannot be called spotted. They may have been born with white ears,
and should have become spotted, but unfortunately in a year's
time became black.

The reason we do not often see the jet black ear
(the ear that was black when born) at a show is, that as a rule this

Imported Gedney Farm Queen of Spots. While a good matron is not a
typical Dalmatian.

dog is most too dark and poorly marked for a show dog and the
owner does not show him. When you get a good spotted eared
dog he is usually very lightly spotted over the body. A very
good spotted dog in body has seldom a good spotted ear. How
many litters are born in which there are not from one to four of the
puppies with one black ear, or both, or with blotches on the
face over the eye. Not many I presume, therefore, I have no

Queen Spot, a good marked one but weak
in head and poor ear carriage. Owned by H.
Fred Lauer.

objections to the black ears, and we should not penalize a dog for
black ears, nor for tan spots on the legs and cheeks, for these we
know to have been proper Dalmatian colorings from the very first
of our information regarding the breed up to the time these English
Clubs were started, and there is no reason why the change has
been made. It is as old as the hills and why now condemn it and
assert that it is wrong. For the past quarter of a century we are
trying to get rid of the black ear and nearly every time a litter is
born, sure enough the black ear is there on some of the litter.
Perhaps the best way to get rid of them would be to cut them off
as was the custom. The ears should be set on rather high
and a size to suit the dog and not appear large and heavy and
hound-like. They should be carried close to the head, be thin and
fine in texture and rather smaller than a Pointer's.

CONFORMATION.

In build, the Dalmatian should be built upon the lines of a
good Pointer. He should have the best of legs and feet, strong
in bone with no more substance than gives the idea that the dog
is strongly built and capable of traveling easily, at a moderately
fast pace for a distance. Therefore he should be solid on his pins,
and one must not lose sight of the fact that this is absolutely
essential in a Dalmatian, for is he not required for road work? Take
that dog of Reinagles; how many of our present-day dogs could
he not beat in an all day run with a team? Many owners think
because they have a dog with a well marked body and no black

A good strong well marked young dog, American bred, that can win in good company. Owned by Indian Neck Farm, Oakdale, L. I.

A poor specimen of a Dalmatian.

ears, with a poor running gear and rat paws they ought to beat everything that comes along. Spotting is all well enough if we are merely to consider the Dalmatian as a dog about the premises, but if we undertake to judge him as a coach dog the principal requirements should be conformation, so he can stand a run with a team, as a coach dog is supposed to do.

The head of a Dalmatian is difficult to describe. It is not like the head of a good pointer, but more on the order of a poor pointer. More like what we might call weak in head in a pointer with a little less squareness and lip, the latter must be clean, fitting the

Nellie, a good conformation bitch used only for breeding purposes and is the mother of many prize winners. Owned by H. Fred. Lauer.

jaws moderately close. The muzzle should be long and yet not too pointy. It should be of good breadth and free from wrinkles.

The eyes should be well apart of medium size, bright sparkling and with more expression than a pointer. Often the Dalmatian is seen with what is called "China," or "Moon," or "Glass," or "Wall" eyes, a peculiarity frequently appearing in all varieties of dogs, or animals that have much white about them, and where white is mixed with black, or what is often called blue. Personally I do not consider this eye detracts from the animal's appearance.

I do not believe any Judge who found this light colored eye in a perfectly marked, good running geared dog would disqualify or even severely handicap him on this account. The Standard says, "Wall eyes" are permissible, and why should they not be, for in Reinagle's dog it can be plainly seen that as old as he is, he has this light colored eye.

The tail should be spotted, but there are many good Dalmatians that do not have any spots on the tail. We have been told that six was the proper number to have on the tail. I wonder why it should be just six. What has the number of spots to do with it?

Litter of puppies out of Nellie ex. Ch. King, this shows the result of breeding a light dog to a dark bitch, the one in the rear having a blotch over the ear and head.

It should be carried with a slight curve upwards and never curled over the back.

The coat should be short, hard, dense and fine, sleek and glossy in appearance, but neither woolly nor silky.

Dogs should weigh from 40 to 50 pounds, not over 50 pounds, and Bitches from 40 to 45 pounds.

General appearance.—The Dalmatian should represent a strong, muscular, active and Pointer shaped dog; symmetrical in outline and by all means free from coarseness and lumber, capable of great endurance, combined with a fair amount of speed.

To do justice, in judging a class of Dalmatians, is a very difficult thing to do, and give satisfaction to all, for, if a Judge goes for spotting—because it is easier than conformation plus spotting—the owner of a dog who has a well built dog, fit to stand the roads, feels aggrieved, and, vice versa, with the man who has the good spotted dog. It is really one of those breeds where the Judge should practice the art of self-defence and resort to point judging; then if he does not put the dog in the proper place to suit the owner, it is the dog's fault not his.

Two puppies, one well marked and the other not. Both puppies have poor ear carriage.

BREEDING.

This variety of the Canine race has but a limited number of breeders and exhibitors. We have had some very enthusiastic breeders the past several years, they seemed to be much taken up with the breed, but all at once they dropped out, and we do not hear of them again. What the cause is we cannot say. Perhaps it is owing to the great difficulty in breeding perfectly marked specimens. Litter after litter may be produced, the progeny of the best parents, without a fairly marked puppy in the whole litter. Some turn out too dark, others too light, some may have heavy black ears, others may, when fully grown look as if a bottle of ink had been emptied over a white cloth and will look more like the color of a grey horse than a spotted dog.

There does not appear to be any rule or guide, by which to breed for perfect markings, I always have bred a light-marked dog to a dark bitch, and vice versa; I have experienced this and find I get the best results by so doing, but with it all some of the pups are entirely too dark. I always said and will say it yet, it is

Litter of puppies bred by H. Fred Lauer out of Nellie ex ch. D'Artagnan. This is the result of breeding a light marked dog to a dark bitch.

only a game of chance when a breeder gets a perfectly marked Dalmatian. Another thing and that is, that many puppies are born deaf. There are a great many Dalmatians to-day that are deaf. Parties purchasing puppies should beware of this, as it is common in Dalmatians and Bull Terriers. Yet another thing, and one that few people except those closely connected with Dalmatians know, that when the puppies are born they come into the world white. Occasionally, they are born with faint spots, or with black ear, or both, or with a large black spot over the side of the face, or a large round spot on top of the head.

This is not as things ought to be in a specimen that is expected to turn out perfect. They should be born perfectly white, and as a rule when perfectly white, they will not be too dark, yet the ears will, as a rule, get pretty black, when the dog is a year old. If the ears stay "spotted" the dog will be very light in markings. If the pups are examined closely the third day, it can be seen where the skin is hairless that the spots come in the skin first. Each day they become darker, the black hair commences to grow in the black spots, and as the black hair grows the white hair in the spots drop out. About the sixth

Good Puppy, 3½ months old in six positions.   Out of Laura ex Kiefer.
Owned by Dr. E. A. Wilson, Salem, W. Va.

or seventh day the spots commence to make themselves apparent. There is a dark ridge along the belly and here the spots can be seen first. The ears spot up and the spots can be seen more plainly where the hair is shortest, on the belly, inside the legs, and about the head.

Those pups that have the black ears and blotches over the side of the face, show the spots sometimes as early as the third day. About the twelfth day, the back becomes darker, the larger spots come out over the entire body, and about the third or fourth week most of the spots, though ill defined, are visible on the body. So the markings continue to develope until the puppy is some four or five months old, at which period all the spots on the body should be very distinct, although he will spot up until a year or fifteen months old. However, the stern or tail generally remains white until about the fourth or fifth month, when if there are to be any spots thereon they should begin to appear.

Still very often they are not visible until the twelfth month, and the quality and appearance of a Dalmatian cannot be told definitely and as a certainty until it is twelve months old, never earlier. So those who are in the habit of purchasing puppies at six weeks, when a Dalmatian is the object, must act accordingly.

A group of Gedney Farm Puppies. None have jet black ears while all are lightly marked. Some of the ears are nearly black.

As a rule, a breeder of good blooded stock will not dispose of his puppies at so early an age. Did he do so, he might for a couple of dollars or so, dispose of what might in the end turn out to be the best dog he ever bred, worth probably several hundred dollars. Often has it occurred, that people having bred Dalmatians, and not knowing that they come into the world "white" have been disgusted, and destroyed the whole litter on this account. I believe there are people to-day who own a Dalmatian, that are not aware of this fact. It would be a hard matter to convice a man who owned a heavily marked dog, but who was not a breeder, that his

43

·dog at one time was perfectly white. Breeding Dalmatians is quite interesting, although discouraging, especially in the markings as they are not like other breeds where one can see as soon as they are born, how they are marked, and pick out the best marked ones and destroy the bad ones. Those which are born with black ears or large blotches on the head are destroyed and the all white ones are kept, and here is where the game of chance comes in, and the chances are you do not get a well marked one.

It is quite an honor for a breeder to breed a Dalmatian, show him, and win the title of "Champion."

Illustration showing litter of four puppies marked very heavily and having the black ears and the black extending over the entire head of one. The Dam of these pups in the rear, is the one with spotted ears. Breeders as a rule destroy these puppies.

The prices of Dalmatian puppies vary a great deal and is due to the breeding and how the puppy is marked, also what kind of head he has, as this is one of the good points. Puppies are sold, both sexes, from $10.00 up to $50.00. Grown dogs are sold from $20.00 up to several hundred dollars. Working "Coach" dogs are sold from $20.00 to $100.00, according to their working ability under a carriage.

44

As to rearing puppies there is quite a disagreement among experts, but this advice will be found to be good, as I have had great success with it. When the puppies are three weeks old try to get them to lap milk, (goat's milk preferred) as it is much better. Do this two or three times daily for a week, when some bread and ground puppy biscuits may be added. Give this diet three or four times a day until eight weeks old, then treat for worms, as all puppies have worms. After this take them off of slop except in the mornings, boil oatmeal or barley with milk for their breakfast. At other times feed them with fine chopped meat and bread, or with vegetables and gravy, and foods that will make growth. Give them a fresh bone to gnaw at, as this aids in digestion. Avoid all sweets such as sugar and candy. Let them have a good yard to run in, and above all avoid a dirty, damp kennel. Good pine sawdust makes a good bedding for puppies, as it is easily kept clean by going through it every day and it is kept dry by changing frequently. Let your puppy have plenty of fresh water, as he likes a good cool drink once in a while just as well as you do. Water that is left standing in the sun all day is bound to upset your dog's condition. Exercise is of great value at all times. Do not take him out on chain—that is not exercise. Turn him loose and let him run. Either exercise before feeding or some time after, as exercise on a full stomach is likely to cause trouble, such as fits, etc.

Follow these directions and your puppy will be kept in good health.

There is no doubt that the spotted dog will be kept as a coach dog or general companion, as he is perfect for this sort of work and his character is now formed by heredity to certain pursuits, it would be a pity to try and divert him to other uses.

Their extremely smart appearance is responsible for their wide distribution in nearly all parts of the world. Their great endurance for long journeys is one of the chief characteristics of the breed, and in fact might say that it is this characteristic that has made the Dalmatian so popular. No matter how great the journey may be they will follow their master as long as they have a leg to stand on. Even puppies only a few months old will follow their master's carriage till their little legs will no longer carry them. Extreme sagacity to follow and protect is certainly bred in them, for they will repel any intruder, man or beast.

That the Dalmatian is making vast strides in America to-day, there can be no doubt, for at the present time, there are more good Dalmatians of both sexes, black and liver spotted, than were to be seen fifteen years ago. This variety still wants more general support, and there is more room for enthusiastic breeders. The year just passed has been notable for the bringing out of some promising specimens, youngsters as well as grown dogs.

Undoubtedly, this breed is rapidly increasing, in both numbers and quality. It is difficult to think of more than very few dogs who were shown in 1896 that could hold their own on the bench to-day.

We have, indeed, gone ahead and improved our Dalmatian to well nigh perfection. There are, however, points in which we have not advanced, and the chief one is that of head, or of the tail marking. It can be seen that all well marked dogs in the illustrations, have white tails with but very few spots.

Much attention has been given to the liver spotted variety, so that there is reason to hope in the future we may see some very good dogs of this color.

Altogether, the prospects of the Dalmatian are decidedly brilliant, and if there were more breeders and coaching men who could be induced to take up this good old time breed we would have in the American bred Dalmatian a dog that holds a prominent place both on the bench and at home.

Kennel Supplies

We have the only safe and reliable Crates made to ship your dogs to and from the dog shows.

They combine lightness strength and durability.

Name and address or the name of kennel painted on top without extra cost.

We carry a full line of sizes on hand for immediate shipment.

We also sell all kinds of Dog Collars, Chains, Leads, Couplers, Brushes, Combs, Snaps; all the latest and best books published.

Austin's, Excelsior, Ideal, Old Grist Mill, Spratt's and Young's Dog and Puppy Cakes.

Glover's, Dent's, Johnson's, Sergeant's, and Spratt's Dog Medicines.

Banner Dog Soap for Washing your Dog. Price, 15 cents; by mail, 20 cents.

Banner Flea and Insect Exterminator kills fleas, roaches, ants, bedbugs, croton bugs, and any other kind of a bug. Price, 15 cents; by mail, 20 cents.

Banner Laxative Tablets are just the thing for house dogs. Price, 10 cents; by mail 2 cents extra.

Banner Sure-Kill is guaranteed to kill worms in puppies and Dogs. The best thing yet. Price, 50 cents, unmailable.

Carrying and sleeping baskets for dogs and cats.

A complete list of supplies will be found in our kennel supply circular, which we send postpaid anywhere. *Send for one.*

Excelsior Wire and Poultry Supply Co.
26 and 28 Vesey Street, New York City

49

SATISFACTION ASSURED

Printed in Great Britain
by Amazon